P9-CLD-983

How are we the same and different?

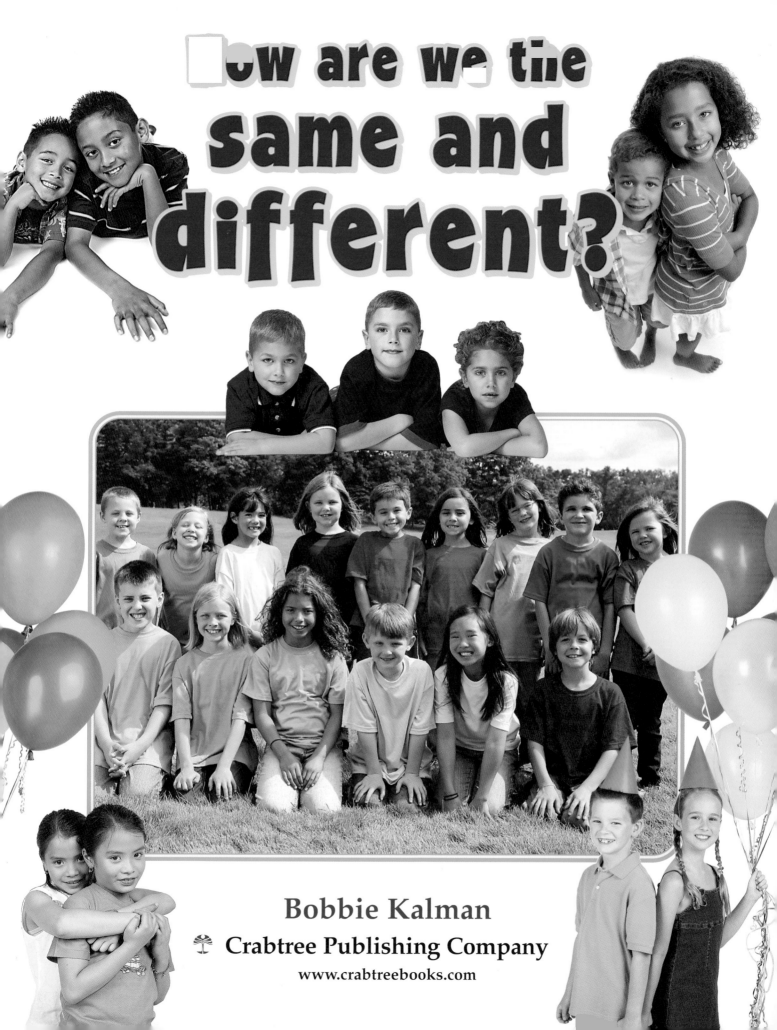

Bobbie Kalman

🌴 Crabtree Publishing Company

www.crabtreebooks.com

Created by
Bobbie Kalman

Inspired by the "Aloha Spirit" of
President Barack Obama.
You help us see the "same" in us all!

Author and
Editor-in-Chief
Bobbie Kalman

Editor
Kathy Middleton

Proofreader
Crystal Sikkens

Photo research
Bobbie Kalman

Design
Bobbie Kalman
Katherine Berti
Samantha Crabtree (cover)

Production coordinator
Katherine Berti

Special thanks to
Francine Jarry for the "Be here now!" text on page 27

Illustrations
Antoinette "Cookie" Bortolon: page 6

Photographs
© iStockphoto.com: back cover, pages 1 (two rows of children),
    5 (bottom), 14 (top), 15 (bottom right), 21 (bottom left),
    25 (top and middle), 26 (top), 28, 29 ("love" and "recycle")
© Bobbie Kalman: page 5 (top)
© Shutterstock.com: front cover, pages 1 (top left and right), 3,
    4, 6, 7 (top right and bottom), 8, 9, 10, 11, 12, 13, 14 (bottom),
    15 (except bottom right), 16, 17, 18, 19, 20, 21 (except bottom
    left), 22, 23, 24 (bottom), 25 (bottom), 26 (bottom), 27,
    29 (except "love" and "recycle"), 30
Other images by Ingram photo objects and StudioGear

Library and Archives Canada Cataloguing in Publication

Kalman, Bobbie
    How are we the same and different? / Bobbie Kalman.

(Our multicultural world)
Includes index.
ISBN 978-0-7787-4633-1 (bound).--ISBN 978-0-7787-4648-5 (pbk.)

    1. Difference (Psychology)--Juvenile literature. 2. Toleration--Juvenile
literature. I. Title. II. Series: Our multicultural world

BF697.K355 2009   j305   C2009-900487-9

Library of Congress Cataloging-in-Publication Data

Kalman, Bobbie.
    How are we the same and different? / Bobbie Kalman.
        p. cm. -- (Our multicultural world)
    Includes index.
    ISBN 978-0-7787-4648-5 (pbk. : alk. paper) -- ISBN 978-0-7787-4633-1
(reinforced library binding : alk. paper)
    1. Difference (Psychology)--Juvenile literature. 2. Toleration--Juvenile
literature. I. Title. II. Series.

BF697.K294 2009
305--dc22

2009002053

Crabtree Publishing Company
www.crabtreebooks.com   1-800-387-7650

Published in Canada
Crabtree Publishing
616 Welland Ave.
St. Catharines, Ontario
L2M 5V6

Published in the United States
Crabtree Publishing
PMB16A
350 Fifth Ave., Suite 3308
New York, NY 10118

Published in the United Kingdom
Crabtree Publishing
White Cross Mills
High Town, Lancaster
LA1 4XS

Published in Australia
Crabtree Publishing
386 Mt. Alexander Rd.
Ascot Vale (Melbourne)
VIC 3032

Contents

Same and different?

We are all different. We look different. Some of us are girls. Some of us are boys. Some of us are tall, and some of us are short. Our faces are not the same. We have different noses, lips, and eyes. Our hair and skin are different, too. In which other ways are we different? How are we the same?

These girls are **quadruplets**. They were born on the same day, look the same, dress the same, and have the same parents. They have different names, they like different foods, and they behave very differently. They are the same and different.

These boys look different, but they go to the same school and play the same sports. They are best friends.

5

The same bodies

People are **living things**. Our bodies are all built the same way. We are **vertebrates**. Vertebrates have **backbones**. Backbones are a row of bones inside the body. We have many other bones that join together to form a **skeleton**. A skeleton supports the body. The bones of the skeleton are covered with muscle, fat, and skin.

What are mammals?

People are also **mammals**. Mammals have hair or fur on their bodies. People have hair. Mammals are born.

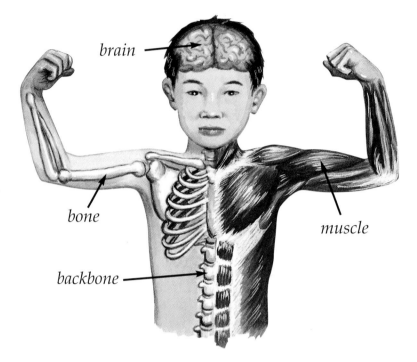

brain

bone

backbone

muscle

The bodies of vertebrates bend. We can move in many ways. This girl is bending backwards!

Is this how babies are born?

Mammals come out live from their mothers' bodies. They do not hatch from eggs the way birds do.

People are primates, too

Primates are very intelligent mammals with big brains. Monkeys and apes are primates, but they are not the same as humans. There are many **species**, or types, of monkeys and apes, but there is only one species of humans. The bodies of people are built the same.

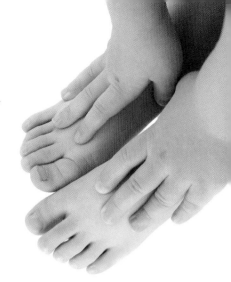

Our big brains allow us to learn anything we want to learn. Our brains also help us make choices in our lives.

The hands and feet of primates have fingers and toes. Our thumbs make it easy for us to grab things. The children below are using their fingers to create an art project.

The eyes of primates are on the front of the face. With our eyes, we can tell how far away things are.

Growing and changing

Hello, world!

Human mothers carry their babies inside their bodies for about nine months. When the babies are born, they cannot look after themselves. Parents look after their children for many years!

Most children have families, but not all families are the same. These children have a mother and father. Some families have more than two parents, and some families have only one parent.

From babies to adults

After we are born, we do not stay the same. Our bodies grow and change. Our thoughts change. Our feelings change. We learn new things every day. We become children and then teenagers. Finally, we are adults. Adults keep changing, too.

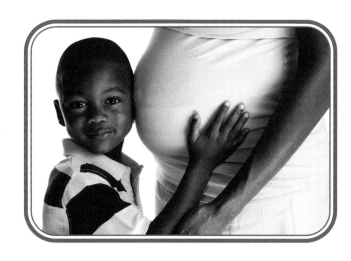

There's a baby in there!

When we are adults, we can have babies. Parents and children become families.

As babies, we learn to crawl at about six months.

From thirteen to nineteen, we are teenagers.

We are children until we are twelve years old.

We learn to walk at about one year. Then we are called toddlers.

9

Earth is our home

We all share the same home—Earth. Earth is the only planet that has air, water, and food. Only Earth has plants, animals, people, and other living things. Everything you eat, breathe, drink, and use comes from Earth. Air, water, plants, animals, people, rocks, and soil are parts of Earth. We need each part to keep living things alive. We are the same because we are all part of Earth!

Earth is one planet, but people have divided it into countries with borders. Imagine looking at Earth from space. You would see no countries or borders!

Attitude of gratitude

Everything Earth gives us is a gift. We can say "Thank you," by showing respect for our gifts. We can stop wasting the things for which we are thankful. We can live our lives with an attitude of **gratitude**. Gratitude is more than just being thankful. It is a way of feeling, acting, and knowing that we are Earth's family. If Earth could speak to us, what would she ask us to do?

Would she tell us that we need to clean the air and water so we will stay healthy? Would she ask us to plant more trees and to throw away less garbage? Would Earth remind us that we are connected to everyone and everything and that we are family? Would Earth remind us that we are part of her?

11

How are we connected?

We are Earth's family, and we are connected to other living and non-living things. We are connected by air, sunshine, water, and food. When we **exhale**, our breath goes into the air and is **absorbed**, or taken in, by plants. Plants then make oxygen, which animals and people breathe. Our breath also contains water **vapor**, which becomes part of the clouds, rain, and the water that animals and people drink. We are connected by sunshine because the energy in sunshine goes into plants and then into our bodies.

There is a gas in air, called **argon**, which never changes or goes away. It was part of the breaths dinosaurs took millions of years ago. It is breathed by us and will be breathed by living things in the future, too. Air connects us to the past and future, as well as to everything on Earth today.

12

Connected to people

We are part of families, friends, schools, cultures, **communities**, and countries. Communities are people who live or belong to a place. We are connected to the world community by the information we share through books, movies, television, and the Internet.

We are connected by our school community.

We are connected to people near and far by the Internet.

What do we need?

Living things need sunshine and fresh air to breathe. We need clean water to drink and healthy food to eat. We need plants and animals and other people. We need families. We need to be part of communities. We need homes to protect us from cold, wet, and hot weather. What else do we need?

This family is having a picnic outdoors. They have many of the things they need. They have food, water, and sunshine. The trees near them are making the air fresh to breathe. Plants have given them the fruits they are eating. They have a dog to keep them company. They have one another.

14

We need homes. This family is moving into a new home.

We need warm clothes in winter and cool clothes in summer. This girl is wearing a snowsuit, hat, boots, and gloves to keep herself warm in the snow.

We have big brains, so we need to learn and use our imagination.

We also need:

- to be healthy
- to feel safe
- ways to have fun
- people who share our ideas and beliefs

We have different cultures

We are different because we come from different **cultures**. Culture is the way we live. It is the clothes we wear, the foods we eat, the languages we speak, the stories we tell, and the ways we celebrate. It is the way we show our imagination through art, music, and writing. When people move from one country to another, they bring their cultures with them. It is fun to learn about the cultures of others. How is your culture different from the cultures of some of your friends?

Do you dress one way at school and another way at home? How many languages do you speak? Which language do you speak at home?

This girl is singing and playing her guitar. She loves music! Music is a part of culture.

This boy takes karate lessons. Sports are part of culture.

What is your favorite kind of music? Do you play a musical instrument? Which one? Do you take part in sports or other activities? What are they?

Celebrations are part of culture. Which are your favorite celebrations? How do you celebrate them?

17

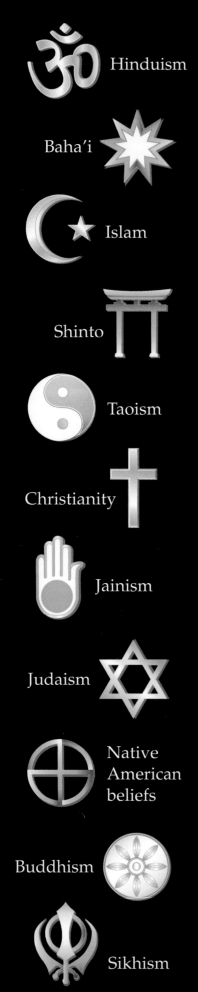

Hinduism

Baha'i

Islam

Shinto

Taoism

Christianity

Jainism

Judaism

Native American beliefs

Buddhism

Sikhism

Different beliefs

We have different beliefs. A **religion** is a belief in a God, gods, or in special ways that help people live better lives. Some religions are shown on the left. Most religions have houses of worship, such as temples, churches, synagogues, or mosques. Many religions also have holy books that people read to learn more about their faiths. Not everyone believes in God or belongs to a religion.

*This family is reading the Bible together. The Bible is the Christian holy book. Christians follow the teachings of Jesus Christ. There are more than 30,000 **denominations**, or different groups, of Christians.*

*Many religions have **symbols**. The symbols on the left are shown beside the religions they represent.*

This Muslim girl is holding the Qur'an, or Koran, the holy book of Islam.

The outside of this beautiful Hindu temple in southern India has many colorful statues of gods.

Some Buddhists spin prayer wheels to send good thoughts and wishes out to the world.

prayer wheel

The girl on the left is using beads to help her pray. People of many religions use prayer beads to keep track of the prayers they are saying.

We have different talents

We can do many things. We can read and write. We can learn to play music and dance. We can play sports. We can draw and paint. Some of us are good at some things. Some of us are good at other things. **Skill** is the ability to do something well with practice. You can learn to do many things well if you work hard enough. Each of us also has special **talents**. Talent is being naturally good at doing the things we love or that interest us. What are your talents?

Are you good at skateboarding, gymnastics, or soccer?
Do you love to do these things?

Do you love to dance?

Are you funny? Were you born into a family of clowns?

Are you a talented magician?

from to

Who are you? Are you just your name, your culture, your beliefs, your talents, or are you something more? Your parents, teachers, or friends may try to tell you who you are, but only you know that answer. The real you is the **unique** person inside you. Unique is one of a kind. Writing a poem about yourself using the letters of the alphabet will help you learn more about yourself. Here are some words you can use to start your poem, but you will likely find better words to describe yourself. Draw pictures to go with your poem. Read your poem often to remember who you are!

A   able, attractive, active, artist

B   beautiful, bold, butterfly

C   creative, child, changing, clown, cool

D   dreamer, different, dancer, doer

E   exciting, energetic, endless

F   fantastic, friend, fun, free, flexible

G   gentle, gifted, grateful, good, genius, great, generous

H   happy, heart, helpful, hopeful

I   intelligent, imaginative, ideal, interesting

J   joyful, just, jewel, jumping jack

K   kind, knowing, kid, kindred

L   loving, light, leader, learner, lavish

M   ME, mindful, magician, more

N nutty, new, noble, natural, nifty, neat

O open, organic, observer, ocean, one

P peaceful, playful, positive, perfect, patient, powerful

Q quick, quality, quiet

R reasonable, rare, respectful, relaxed, real

S sunny, silly, soft, sane, spirited, safe

T talented, true, trusting, trustworthy

U unusual, unique, understanding

V valuable, vivacious, versatile, visionary

W wise, worker, well, wonderful, wishful

X eXtraordinary, eXciting, eXtreme, eXact

Y young, yes, YOU

Z zany, zealous

23

Yes, we can!

We are more alike than we are different, but sometimes we see only our differences. We may make fun of others because they do not dress like we do or because their beliefs are different. When we forget that we are connected, we pull away from one another. We may even hurt one another. There are many problems in the world today. We need to change the way we think, act, and live. When we work together, we can do anything. Yes, we can!

How can you and your classmates work together to make this world a happier place?

When we do not feel connected, we hurt one another. We hurt one another with words and by our actions. We hurt others only when we are angry or afraid. Happy people do not hurt others.

What is the common good?

The **common good** is the best possible life for everyone on Earth. You can help change the world by working for the common good in your family, school, and community.

A better life

You and your classmates can create a better life at school. Have a meeting each morning and talk about how you can practice the important ideas in the box below. At the end of the day, write down all the good things that have happened that day. Together, repeat your goal, "Our lives are good! We are all good!"

Respect: Respect is showing that you admire others, even if you do not share their beliefs or traditions.

Non-violence: Negative thoughts, words, and actions hurt you and others! Before you say or do something, think about whether your words or actions might hurt someone.

Kindness: You can show kindness by smiling, being friendly, giving compliments, and helping others.

Gratitude: When you live your life in gratitude, you feel very thankful. Write down three things each day for which you are grateful and say "Thank you" often to people.

United: When we work as a team, we feel connected. We can do anything!

Unlimited: There are no limits to what you can achieve. "You can do it!"

Generosity: Share what you have. Share your good thoughts, too. Good thoughts are gifts to yourself and others.

Service: Helping others is very important if you want a better life. In which ways can you volunteer to help right now?

Forgive: Do not stay angry!

Love: Love heals. Treat everyone the same as you treat the people you love.

Joy: Joy is feeling very happy. It comes from inside. How can we be happy?

How can we be  ?

We all want to be happy, but we are different in how happy we can be. Some people are happy most of the time, no matter what problems they have. Other people find it hard to be happy. A person who has everything he or she needs may not be as happy as a person who has very little. Good things that happen to people may make them happy for a while, but true happiness can only come from inside. We can be much happier if we change a few things in our lives and practice them every day.

1. Breathe!

We can change how we feel by changing how we breathe. Close your eyes and **focus**, or think only about, your breath. Inhale, or take in, a big breath of air through your nose. Push that air all the way down to your belly. Feel your belly fill with air. Then exhale, or push the air out through your nose.

2. Happy in, happy out

When you exhale, breathe out any sad thoughts or feelings. When you inhale again, think of something that makes you feel happy. Fill your body with that happy breath. Then send that happy feeling out to the world. Your good wishes will travel with each happy breath you exhale.

3. Quiet time

When you spend time being quiet, your mind becomes clearer. You feel more in touch with the real you. You become stronger and less afraid. To keep your mind on good thoughts, repeat these statements or ones that you have made up. "I am good. I am unique. I am happy to be me. I love myself and others."

4. Be here now!

The past is just a memory, and the future is yet to come. The present is a gift to me, to you, and everyone. This is a beautiful moment. Now is the perfect time, to be where I am and to do what I'm doing. This is the perfect day! Don't think about the past or future. Be happy right now!

Making a difference

We have different talents and dreams, but each one of us also has a **purpose**. Our purpose is why we are here. No matter what challenges life has given us, there is always someone who can use our help. Making a difference in the lives of others can make a huge difference in our lives, too! People remember us for the way we have treated others. How will people remember you?

Lend a helping hand.

Hug a baby or a pet and feel the love in your heart. Treat others with that kind of love.

Send loving thoughts to others with each breath you exhale.

LOVE

Help your parents by looking after your younger brothers or sisters.

How can you and your friends work together to help Earth? Start with the 3Rs: reduce, reuse, and

RECYCLE

Different is beautiful!

We have different faces, different talents, and different dreams. We are like the pieces of a patchwork quilt. If all the pieces were the same, the quilt would be boring. Can you imagine how boring the world would be if we were all the same? Everyone would do the same things, like robots. There is no one exactly like any of us, yet we are all the same! We are all the same because we are all different, and different is beautiful!

Glossary

Note: Some boldfaced words are defined where they appear in the book.

exhale To breathe out

focus To pay attention to something

living thing A person or thing that moves, grows, changes, and dies

primates A group of mammals with large brains, including humans, chimpanzees, and monkeys

quadruplets Four people born at the same time to the same parents

skeleton The set of bones that supports a person or an animal's body

skill The ability to do something well with practice

species A group of similar living things that can make babies with one another

symbol Something that stands for something else

talent A natural ability to do something well

unique One of a kind

vapor Water that has become a part of air after it was heated

vertebrate A type of animal that has a backbone; people are vertebrates, too

Index

Further reading

These books will help you learn more about how we are the same and different. For more information about the books, look for them in your library or go to **www.crabtreebooks.com**.

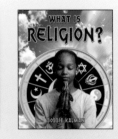

Other books to read in **Our Multicultural World** series: *What is Religion?; What is Culture?; We are the Earth*. Reading level: grades 3–4.

The Lands, Peoples, and Cultures series by **Bobbie Kalman**: Learn about how the people who live in these countries are the same as, or different than, you: Afghanistan, Argentina, Australia, Brazil, Canada, China, Cuba, Egypt, El Salvador, England, France, Germany, Greece, India, Iran, Iraq, Ireland, Israel, Italy, Jamaica, Japan, Mexico, Nigeria, Pakistan, Peru, Philippines, Puerto Rico, Russia, South Africa, Spain, Sweden, and Vietnam. Reading level: grades 4–5.

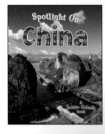
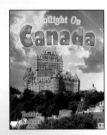

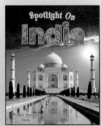

Spotlight On My Country series by **Bobbie Kalman**: This series includes: Australia, Canada, China, Mexico, India, Peru, and the United States of America. Reading level: grades 2–3.

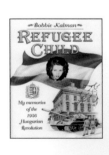

Refugee Child is the exciting story of author Bobbie Kalman's experiences during the Hungarian Revolution, her middle-of-the-night escape across the border to Austria, and her life as a refugee and immigrant. Bobbie overcame many obstacles on her way to becoming an author of hundreds of children's books. Being a refugee and immigrant can make you feel very different from everyone else. Kindness, respect, and love make the differences go away. Reading level: grades 4–5.

Celebrations in My World series explores the history and traditions of major celebrations around the world, including: *Christmas, Easter, Chinese New Year, Day of the Dead, Earth Day, Halloween, Passover, Thanksgiving, Diwali, Cinco de Mayo, Ramadan, Hanukkah, Kwanzaa, Martin Luther King, Jr. Day,* and *Constitution Day*. Reading level: grades K–2.

 Printed in the U.S.A.—CG